Purple Ronnie's

Little Thoughts about

DADS

by Purple Ronnie

First published 2003 by Boxtree
an imprint of Pan Macmillan Ltd
Pan Macmillan, 20 New Wharf Road, London N1 9RR
Basingstoke and Oxford
Associated companies throughout the world
www.panmacmillan.com

ISBN 0 7522 1547 7

9 8

A CIP catalogue record for this book is available from
the British Library.

Text by Giles Andreae
Illustrations by Janet Cronin
Printed and bound in Hong Kong

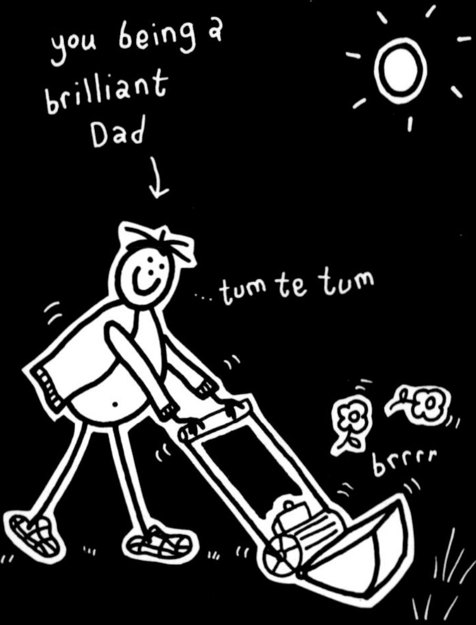
you being a brilliant Dad
...tum te tum
brrrr

a poem for
↓
My Smashing Dad

Your tummy's spreading
out a bit
Your hair is getting thinner
But none of that's
important

Cos I say you're a
winner!

Remember

Dads are hardly ever
at their best first
thing in the morning

Special Tip

From time to time
Dads love to be
told they're a hero

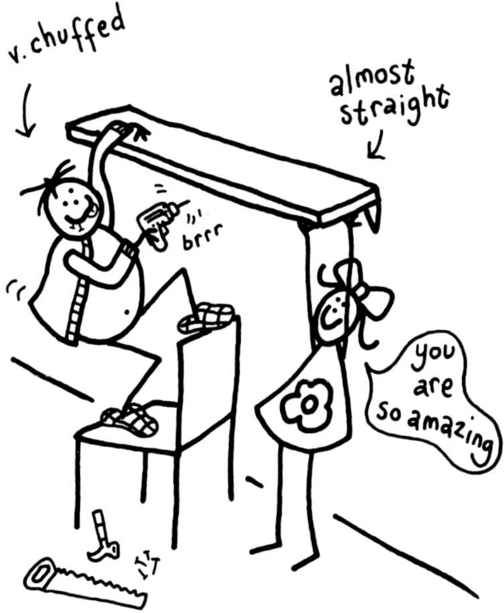
v. chuffed
almost straight
brrr
you are so amazing

a poem for a

Star Dad

Has anyone recently told you

How totally smashing you are

If not here's a message to tell you

That this person thinks you're a star

Dads and the Lav

Most Dads love nothing more than a really good session on the lav

Sometimes you can forget just how useful Dads really are

a poem about my

Groovy Dad

Sometimes people's fathers
Can be boring, dull or rude

But my Dad is fantastic
Cos he's such a groovy
dude

Dads and Gadgets

Dads can hardly ever resist a really good new gadget

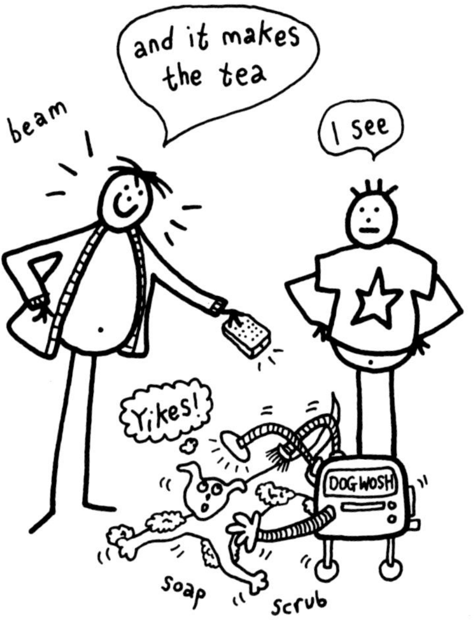
and it makes the tea
beam
I see
Yikes!
DOG WOSH
soap
scrub

Smooth Dads

Beware — What your Dad thinks is smooth is hardly ever the same as what your friends think is smooth

oh yes, I was a bit of a ladies man - cocktail, Señorita?
umm...
cringe
strain
horrid red trousers

a poem for
↓
My Dad

This poem is specially to
tell you

The reason why you are so
great

You're not only brilliant at
being my Dad

You're also a really top
mate

Warning :-

Dads can be the most embarrassing dancers ever

Sporty Dads

The great thing about Sporty Dads is you always know what to get them for their birthday

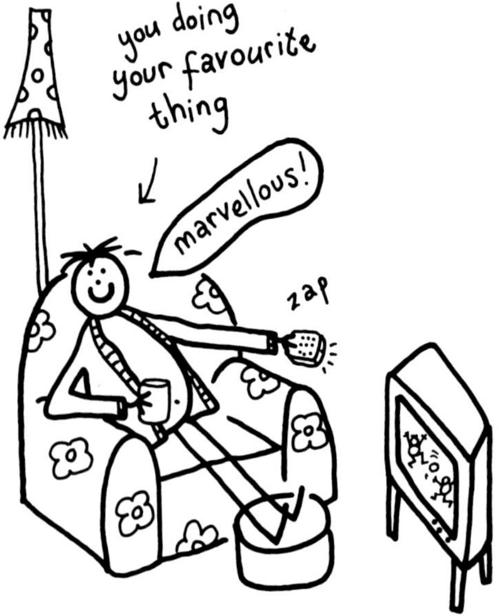
you doing
your favourite
thing
marvellous!
zap

a poem for ↓

My Lovely Dad

Some Dads play golf at
the weekend

Or sail in their boats out
at sea

But others just love to
laze out in a chair

And watch loads of sport
on TV

Some Dads just can't accept that they're not as young as they used to be

Competitive Dads

Some Dads always want to be the best at everything

a poem for

My Fab Dad

Sometimes as Dads become
older
Their hair starts to vanish
away
Their tummies go saggy
Their bottoms go baggy
But you just get better
each day

Warning:-

As Dads get older they start growing hair in the weirdest places

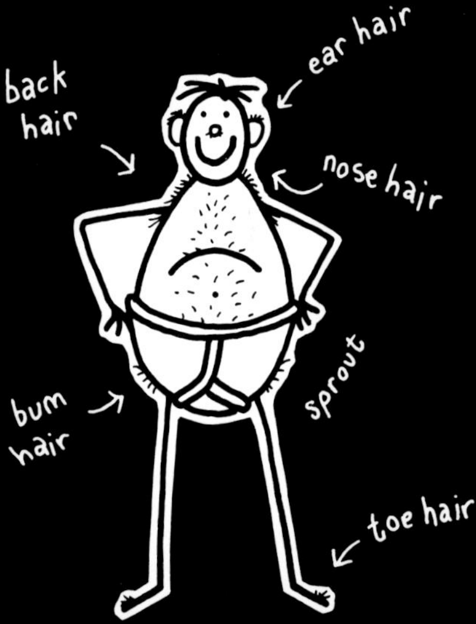
back hair
ear hair
nose hair
bum hair
sprout
toe hair

Special Tip

Even Dads need hugs

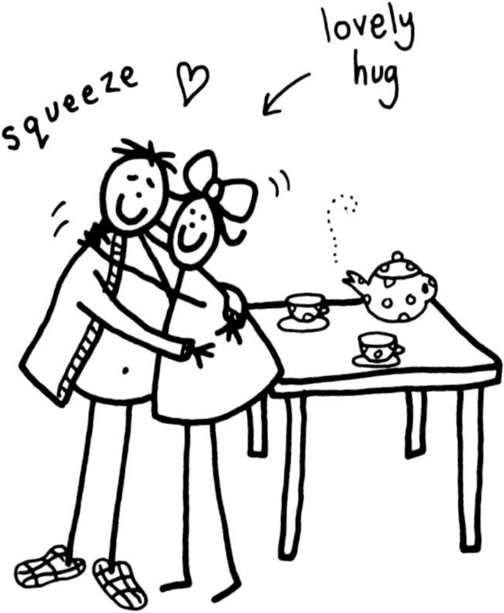
squeeze
lovely hug

a poem for
↓

My Perfect Dad

Some fathers can be
boring

And some can be quite
mad

But I am really lucky

Cos you're the perfect
Dad!

Interesting Point

Although Mums
hardly ever fart,
Dads hardly ever stop

Fact :-

All Dads are really just little boys at heart

a poem for ↓

My Dad

If all the world's Dads
got together
To enter a Super Dad test
I'm sure you'd be voted the
winner
Cos you are by miles
the best